RALPH
VAUGHAN WILLIAMS
a pictorial biography

RALPH VAUGH

a pictoria

John E. Lunn and

OXFORD UNIVERSITY PRES

AN WILLIAMS

biography

UrsulaVaughanWilliams

Ion New York Toronto 1971

OXFORD UNIVERSITY PRESS
Ely House, London W1

ISBN 0 19 315420 X

Glasgow New York Toronto Melbourne Wellington
Cape Town Salisbury Ibadan Nairobi Dar Es Salaam Lusaka Addis Ababa
Bombay Calcutta Madras Karachi Lahore Dacca
Kuala Lumpur Singapore Hong Kong Tokyo

We wish to thank all those named below who have kindly allowed us to reproduce photographs appearing in this book: Aberdeen Journals Ltd.: p. 110 (with some of the choir); Alburtus—Yale News Bureau: p. 99 (Luther Noss presenting the prize); Arnold Ashby: p. 95 (Gypsy Hill Training College Summer School); Associated Newspapers Ltd.: p. 79, p. 86 (with C. Day Lewis), p. 104 (with Sir John Barbirolli at rehearsals—2 plates at top of page); Erich Auerbach, F.R.P.S.: p. 115, p. 116, p. 117, p. 118 (after performance *Ninth Symphony*); Edmund Barkworth: p. 3 (the hall at Tanhurst); Baumann: p. 61 (at the coronation of King George VI); Berrow's Newspapers Ltd.: p. 95 (with Herbert Howells and David Willcocks); Miss Sybilla Bonham Carter: p. 48 (Ralph as audience); Sir Adrian Boult: p. 74 (wedding of Sir Adrian Boult's stepdaughter); Bristol Evening Post: p. 82 (Dr Walter Stanton presenting Ralph to the Chancellor); W. J. Brunell: p. 61 (RVW conducting the band of the 2nd Battalion); Rev. John Burnaby: p. 43 (Old King Cole); M. E. Calthrop: p. 60 (Piper's Guild Summer School); E. C. Cawte: p. 100 (with Douglas Kennedy); Charterhouse: p. 10 (concert programme), p. 11 (both plates), p. 12 (all three plates), p. 13; Cheltenham Newspaper Co. Ltd.: p. 100 (at a party in the Pittville Gardens); Mrs Gordon Clark: p. 56 (with Hervey; with Adrian Boult; with Judge Gordon Clark); Leslie Collier, F.I.I.P.: p. 111 (with Alan Frank and Grigor Piatigorski), p. 113 (at the party following the concert; Ralph's 85th birthday concert); Howard Coster: p. 63; H. E. Crooks: p. 83 (RVW with conductors); Charles Cudworth: p. 107 (croquet at the Finzis' house); Daily Express: p. 89 (both plates), p. 105 (at a party); L. Ducock: p. 80 (conducting the teachers' course); Miss Ada and Miss Gertrude Durrant: p. 55 (Three Choirs Festival); Ealing Films: p. 71; Elgar Birthplace Trust: p. 55 (with W. H. Reed); Elliott and Fry: p. 21 (George E. Moore), p. 22 (Sir Hubert Parry), p. 45, p. 93 (Sir Gilmour Jenkins); English Folk Dance and Song Society: p. 49 (with a Morris dancer), p. 53 (the opening of Cecil Sharp House), p. 100 (addressing the AGM of the E.F.D.S.S. 1955), p. 114 (a party at Cecil Sharp House); Evening World: p. 82 (after the ceremony); David Farrell: p. 109; Miss Herma Fiedler: p. 72; Raymond Fowler: p. 101 (2 plates; pony ride up the hill, Delphi); Fox Photos: p. 64 (Sir Henry Wood's 75th birthday); Douglas Glass: p. 77, p. 114 (at Hanover Terrace); The Gloucester Journal: p. 107 (Garden Party at Gloucester); Mrs Grigg: p. 52 (Ralph); The Guardian: p. 88 (rehearsal at the Free Trade Hall), p. 105 (at a rehearsal of the Eighth Symphony); The Guardian Journal: p. 114 (receiving an Honorary Degree); Mrs G. M. Harvey: p. 85 (with Sir Malcolm Sargent and Larry Adler); Mrs Molly Hodge: p. 97 (by the swimming pool at the Biltmore Hotel); Miss Imogen Holst: p. 42 (all four plates); Frank Hollins: p. 102 (picnic at the top of the Lauteret pass); Ideal Studios Ltd.: p. 49 (RVW in a group photo); Sir Gilmour Jenkins: p. 81 (all four plates); p. 93 (Hanover Terrace 1953); Mrs Michael Kennedy: p. 119; Liam Kennedy: p. 102 (Ralph in group photo); Brendan Kerney: p. 96 (the choristers; rehearsing in the Cathedral; rehearsing in the Cathedral with David Willcocks); Keystone Press Agency Ltd.: p. 92 (London rehearsal with the Boyd Neel Orchestra); Eric L. King: p. 95 (with Herbert Howells and Leslie Woodgate); Miss Lasker: p. 54 (singing in the garden of the Bishop's Palace); Layland-

Ross Ltd.: p. 92 (the party at Nottingham); Miss Barbara Levick: p. 101 (the Acropolis, Athens); Sydney Loeb: p. 46 (Ralph 1921); Dr John E. Lunn: p. 20 (the house at Seatoller 1968), p. 26 (the Vicarage); The Raymond Mander & Joe Mitchenson Theatre Collection: p. 43 (Hugh the Drover); The Mansell Collection: p. 59 (Hervey); The Marchioness of Aberdeen: p. 110 (excursions near Haddo—2 plates); Mrs M. Meredith: p. 41 (Fancy Dress Ball; Ralph and Adeline); Somerset Murray: p. 62; The Musical Times: p. 46 (Gustav Holst 1921); William Narraway: p. 69; The National Monuments Record (Crown Copyright): p. 10 (Field House); p. 25; The National Portrait Gallery, London: p. 2 (Erasmus Darwin); p. 108, p. 33; E. J. Newman: p. 101 (at the temple, Sunion); Ralph Nicholson: p. 94 (with Gerald Finzi—2 plates); Oxford Mail & Times: p. 83 (after a performance of *The Serenade to Music*); Oxford University Press: p. 111 (with Leopold Stokowski); Photo Science Studios: p. 97 (conducting the Cornell Symphony Orchestra); Popperfoto: p. 74 (presenting the RPS's gold medal to Sir John Barbirolli), p. 87 (with Sir Arthur Bliss), p. 106 (with Professor Woodworth and Sir Adrian Boult); The Press Association Ltd.: p. 46 (rehearsing at the Royal Opera House), p. 112 (starting for a holiday in Austria); Mrs Frances Powers: p. 60 (Conductors' conference); Radio Times Hulton Picture Library: p. 64 (Sir Stanley Marchant), p. 78-9 (three plates), p. 90 (both plates); Rex Features Ltd.: p. 118 (rehearsal for the *Ninth Symphony*); The Royal College of Music, London: p. 16, p. 17 (a singing classroom; a violin classroom; Sir George Grove), p. 22 (the library at the RCM), p. 48 (Sir Hugh Allen); The Salvation Army: p. 99 (with General Wilfrid Kitching and others); Evan Senior: p. 87 (with Agnes Nicholls); Mrs Gordon Stafford: p. 93 (Crispin and Friskin); The Staffordshire Sentinel Newspaper: p. 54 (Gustav Holst), p. 104 (bottom of page); Harry Steggles: p. 38 (motor ambulance at Ecoivres); Mrs Alice Sumsion: p. 51 (The White Gates), p. 50; Sun Photographs: p. 88 (with the Hallé Orchestra); Thomson Newspapers Ltd.: p. 106 (with Florent Schmitt), p. 111 (with Arthur Benjamin); Stephen Townroe: p. 65 (with Jean Stewart; with Gerald Finzi and Isidore Schwiller); United Press International UK Ltd.: p. 84 (leaving Westminster Abbey), p. 86 (replying to a speech); Mrs Ralph Vaughan Williams: p. 4 (all three plates), p. 5 (all three plates), p. 24 (Ralph at Bolzano), p. 49 (Gustav Holst), p. 52 (with Adeline; with Elizabeth Darbishire; haymaking; riding), p. 65 (with Harry Steggles; the spire of St. Martin's Church), p. 73 (with Frederick Thurston and the Finzis; at the White Gates), p. 84 (at Chartres; at Mont St. Michel; at Llanthony Abbey), p. 94 (holiday in Italy—2 plates), p. 96 (with Canon and Mrs. Briggs), p. 102 (with Frank Hollins), p. 106 (with Arnold Van Wyk); Vogue (Ph: Norman Parkinson): p. 76; Ernest Willoughby: p. 55 (at Bryn Mawr; with Ernest Willoughby at Bryn Mawr); The Yorkshire Weekly Post: p. 32; the BBC: p. 68 (at the Royal Albert Hall), p. 85 (after the performance); Gloucester Journal: p. 56 (Three Choirs Festival); Edmond Kapp: p. 35; Trustees of the British Museum: p. 31 ('Bushes and Briars'); Bristol United Press: p. 82; Kenneth Collins: p. 58; Karsh of Ottawa: p. 121; Dudley Styles: p. 2 (John Williams), p. 70; Wedgwood Museum Trust: p. 2 (Josiah Wedgwood).

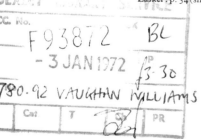
Printed in Great Britain
by Latimer Trend & Co. Ltd., Whitstable.

Designed by Peter Powell

Introduction

A composer's life is his music, but he is also a human being belonging to a particular place and time. His art may transcend his circumstances, but the roots from which he has grown and his place in life nourish and shape that art, and show us the man from whose work we have already discovered both mind and heart.

Pictures can bring these circumstances to life more vividly than anything, and that is why John Lunn and I have brought together the material in this book. It started with a coincidence: just when the usual collection of old snapshots and photographs from the family albums had to be put into some sort of chronological order and tidied up, John Lunn appeared with his own collection of photographs of R.V.W. This collection, the result of a methodical search, was gathered from newspaper offices and photographers' studios as well as from the composer's friends. Once the two lots were amalgamated we found we had a pictorial record of a lifetime, a fragment of history.

We are indebted to many people for their help, not only for finding photographs for us and giving or lending them, but also for identifying people or recalling occasions when the pictures were taken.

I have written a short biographical note to cover the early years. After that the captions carry on the story while lists of the main works will remind readers of what the composer was writing at the time. We think it important that someone who was well known in his later years, as R.V.W. was, should also be remembered as a musical child, as a student, and as a young man struggling to make his way in his profession. These photographs record moments of time, aspects of appearance, but the essence of Ralph Vaughan Williams's being is in the music that was the work of his life.

U.V.W.

Chronology

1872 Born 12 October at Down Ampney, Gloucestershire
1890 Entered Royal College of Music as a student: September
1892 Entered Trinity College, Cambridge. Continued weekly lessons at the RCM
1894 Mus B Cantab
1895 BA (Cantab). Re-entered Royal College of Music. Became organist of St. Barnabas, South Lambeth
1897 Married Adeline Fisher, 9 October. Went to Berlin and studied with Max Bruch
1898 Obtained FRCO diploma by examination
1899 Passed Mus D Cantab examination; took the degree May 1901
1902 Gave University Extension Lectures (and wrote articles for *The Vocalist*) for several years
1903 Started to collect folk-songs. Wrote the articles on *Conducting* and *Fugue* for Grove's Dictionary (1904)
1904 Started work on editing the English Hymnal
1905 First Leith Hill Festival
1908 Studied with Ravel in Paris
1909 *On Wenlock Edge*; *The Wasps*
1910 *A Sea Symphony*, first performed at Leeds Festival *Tallis Fantasia*, first performance at Three Choirs Festival, Gloucester
1912 Conducted and arranged music for Benson's seasons of plays at Stratford-upon-Avon
1914 *A London Symphony* first performed Enlisted as a private in the RAMC
1916 Posted to France and later Salonika
1917 Commissioned as a Lieut. RGA Posted to France
1918 Served in France. Appointed Director of Music, First Army BEF
1919 Demobilized. Appointed Professor of Composition, RCM. Hon D Mus, Oxford
1921 Appointed Conductor of the Bach Choir
1922 *A Pastoral Symphony*. First visit to America
1922 *Mass in G minor*
1924 *Hugh the Drover*
1925 *Flos Campi*; *Concerto Accademico*
1926 *Sancta Civitas*
1928 Resigned from Bach Choir
1929 Moved to Dorking. *Sir John in Love*
1930 *Job*. First performance at Norwich Festival
1931 *Job* staged in London
1932 Gave the Mary Flexner Lectures at Bryn Mawr College (Penn)
1933 *Piano Concerto*
1934 Death of Gustav Holst
1935 *Symphony No 4 in F minor*. Created OM

1936 *The Poisoned Kiss*; *Dona Nobis Pacem*; *Five Tudor Portraits*
1937 *Riders to the Sea*
1938 *Serenade to Music*
1939 Film music, war work, lecturing, writing
1943
1943 *Symphony in D major (No 5)*
1944 *Oboe Concerto*
1945 *Thanksgiving for Victory*
1948 *Symphony in E minor (No 6)*
1950 *Folk Songs of the Four Seasons. Concerto Grosso*
1951 *Pilgrim's Progress* Adeline Vaughan Williams died, 10 May
1952 *Romance for Harmonica*; *An Oxford Elegy*
1953 *Sinfonia Antartica (No 7)* Married Ursula Wood (daughter of Major General Sir Robert Lock, KBE, CB, and Lady Lock) widow of Lieut. Colonel Michael Forrester Wood Moved to London
1954 *Tuba Concerto*; *Hodie*; *Violin Sonata* Lectured at Cornell University, NY. Lecture tour across USA
1956 *Symphony in D minor (No 8)*
1958 *Symphony in E minor (No 9)* Died on 26 August of coronary thrombosis

Family background

On his father's side Ralph Vaughan Williams came from a family distinguished in law. His great-grandfather, John Williams, came to London from Carmarthen at the end of the eighteenth century and became a Serjeant at Law. He married Mary Clarke of Foribridge in Staffordshire and their second son, Edward Vaughan Williams, became a judge, the first to be given the title of Judge of Common Pleas. His wife was Jane Bagot, and they had six sons, as well as daughters who all died as children. Of the sons two followed their father in the profession of the law, and two, Edward and Ralph's father Arthur, were ordained and became country clergymen.

On his mother's side Ralph's forebears were scientists and craftsmen. Among them were Erasmus Darwin, physician and poet, friend of Dr Johnson and a member of the Lunar Society: and Josiah Wedgwood the potter, a Fellow of the Royal Society. The families of Darwin and Wedgwood frequently intermarried and Ralph's grandfather, the third Josiah, married Caroline Darwin, an elder sister of Charles Darwin. Charles Darwin himself was a frequent visitor to Leith Hill Place, a house the Wedgwoods bought in 1847, and he enlisted the help of his three young nieces, the Wedgwood daughters, in his work on earthworms and in collecting botanical specimens for him.

When the second daughter, Margaret, married Arthur Vaughan Williams he took her to Down Ampney on the borders of Gloucestershire and Wiltshire, where he had recently accepted the living. Judging by letters from the vicar he had served earlier as curate at Bemerton in Wiltshire, once George Herbert's parish, and by the journal kept by the schoolmaster at Down Ampney he was a much loved and well-trusted man with a great affection for the children of the parishes in which he worked. He died when Ralph was only two, and Margaret took their three children back to Leith Hill Place where they spent their childhood.

top John Williams,
Serjeant at Law
1757-1810
left Josiah Wedgwood
1730-1795
right Erasmus Darwin
1731-1802

John Williams of Job's Well, Carmarthen, was said to have 'extraordinary powers of memory and excellent understanding' as well as 'patient and persevering application'. All were qualities inherited by his great-grandson. The portrait of Josiah Wedgwood by Sir Joshua is very like Ralph in later life, particularly the broad forehead, bushy eyebrows, and clear eyes. From Erasmus Darwin he inherited his long and sensitive hands

The hall at Tanhurst

The Three Sisters

Tanhurst stands on the south-western slope of Leith Hill and is the nearest house to Leith Hill Place, separated only by a wood where the Wedgwoods planted rhododendrons and azaleas. There is a family tradition that when Sir Edward Vaughan Williams was asked why he had chosen the Leith Hill district for his country home he answered 'Because it is so full of charming young heiresses!' The Vaughan Williamses and Wedgwoods became friends, as did their children.

3

Arthur Vaughan Williams 1834-1875
Ralph's father. Third son of Sir Edward and
Lady Vaughan Williams, ordained 1860,
vicar of Down Ampney, Gloucestershire,
1868-1875

The Vicarage of Down Ampney, birthplace
of the two younger children of the marriage,
Margaret (Meggie) and Ralph (12 October
1872). The eldest, Hervey, was born at Leith
Hill Place.

All Saint's Church at Down Ampney

Margaret Susan Wedgwood. 1843-1937
Ralph's mother

Leith Hill Place, south front

Coldharbour Church
Where Arthur and Margaret were married,
22 February 1866

Front row, Mark Cook, gardener, Sarah Wager, the children's nurse (of whom Ralph was particularly fond), Annie Longhurst, and Joseph Berry. The butler, Phillips, is in the back row. The indoor servants are dressed unconventionally for the period, and they were all remembered as interesting personalities by the family they stayed with throughout their working lives.

Family background

'Margaret . . . seems a capital mother, very intelligent and yet firm enough to carry off little Ralph remorselessly when he screams, which he does on slight provocation' wrote Emma Darwin to her son in 1875. Whether the screams were caused by temper or by boredom we shall never know, but a year later Ralph had learned to read, and by the time he was six he had started to compose. He had a toy theatre for which he wrote overtures for plays acted by his small, toy dogs. His Aunt Sophy helped him to study musical theory and to her he dictated his answers for a correspondence course organized by Edinburgh University which he took when he was eight. He played duets with Hervey and Meggie, and when he was seven started violin lessons. These were continued while he was at his preparatory school, and there his pianoforte teacher, Mr A. C. West, gave him his first introduction to the music of Bach.

Margaret read aloud and the children enjoyed fairy tales, poetry, adventure stories, and the plays of Shakespeare as well as the usual indoor pastimes of painting and making scrap books. They sailed toy boats, rode ponies, and tobogganed on the steep slope of the garden. There were holidays abroad, and when he was ten Ralph, with Hervey, climbed the tower at Rouen Cathedral before the whole party went on to stay at Mont St Michel. From this holiday sprang his great interest in architecture.

In 1887 Ralph went to Charterhouse. He joined the choir and the school orchestra, changed from violin to viola, and he had organ lessons. He was still composing as well as arranging music for any available instruments in the holidays. Although he did not care for school games he played both croquet and tennis at home, read a great deal and went to any concerts he could.

Hervey and Meggie. 1873

Hervey and Meggie. 1876

Ralph. 1876

Hervey. 1877

Coffee, the children's dog

Ralph. 1880

8

Hervey. 1885

Ralph. 1885

Meggie. 1885

School group,
Field House. 1886
(Ralph 7th from the left
in the 2nd row from the
back)

In 1883 Ralph followed Hervey to Field House (now
St Aubyn's), a preparatory school at Rottingdean
near Brighton. Ralph continued his violin lessons and
became interested in mathematics. He played games
without much pleasure, but he liked the open country
and the bare hillsides of the South Downs.

Programme of a 'Musical and Dramatic Entertainment' given at Field House on 15 December 1886

Far right Concert programme

PART I.

PROLOGUE	W. Wakeford, Esq.
A. W. CHURCHILL.	
CHORUS... ... "The Old Brigade." ...	O. Barri.
VIOLIN TRIO	
R. V. WILLIAMS, H. PHILLIPS, H. G. LEWIN.	
TRIO ... ... Cradle Song.... ...	Taubert.
VIOLIN SOLO	Gounod.
R. V. WILLIAMS.	
PART SONG ... "The Legend of the Bells." ...	From Les Cloches de Corneville.
BALLAD (with chorus) "The Primrose." ...	F. Abt.
A. W. EDGELOW, H. O. CLARKE, R. T. GODMAN.	
TRIO ... ... "Evening."	H. Smart.
CANTATA ... "ROBIN HOOD." ...	Lerey.
RECITATION ... From "The Heir at Law." ...	Colman.
W. T. SUTTHERY, Esq.	
VIOLIN SOLO ... ... Scotch Airs.	Sainton.
W. M. QUIRKE, Esq.	
Accompanist - - - - W. W. HEWITT, Esq.	

MUSICAL SKETCH:

A RURAL HOLIDAY,

C. T. WEST, Esq.

CHARTERHOUSE,

SUNDAY, AUGUST 5TH, 1888.

Programme.

PIANOFORTE DUET { Rondo from Quartet in C minor }	...	Spohr.
H. W. C. ERSKINE AND J. G. S. MELLOR.		
SONG ... "The Chorister" ...	...	Sullivan.
B. G. BRANSTON.		
TRIO ... ... in G	R. V. Williams.	
H. V. HAMILTON { B. K. R. WILKINSON R. V. WILLIAMS } S. MASSINGBERD.		
SONG ... "There is a green hill far away"	Gounod.	
MR. L. MARSHALL.		
PIANOFORTE SOLO } ... Phantaisie in A ...	...	Bach.
MR. ROBINSON.		
SONG ... "I dreamt I was in Heaven"	H. V. Hamilton.	
B. G. BRANSTON.		
QUARTET ... ... No. 5	...	Haydn.
J. E. BIDWELL, A. G. G. COWIE, T. SHAW, C. M. RAYNER.		
AIR ... ... From the "Creation" ...	Haydn.	
MR. BODE.		
DUET FOR TWO PIANOFORTES } Sonata in D	Mozart.	
H. V. HAMILTON AND N. G. SMITH.		

Field House

'One of the most astounding events of my school musical life took place when Hamilton and I decided to give a concert of our own compositions. It was my task to approach Dr Haig Brown, the Headmaster, for leave to use the school hall. Dr Haig Brown was a formidable man, and in later life I should never have dared to make the request, but leave was obtained, and we gave the concert, and it was attended by several of the masters and their wives, and even some of the boys.' R.V.W. in *The Carthusian* December 1952.

Concert at Charterhouse

Below Charterhouse. 1888

right Charterhouse group. 1889. Ralph as Head Monitor of Robinites.

centre Group. 1889 (Ralph, 4th from left, front row). Hervey as Monitor

foot Charterhouse Cadet Force. 1889 (Ralph, extreme right, 3rd row)

Duffey
Hamilton H V   } 1.2.3   idle
                              no Impos.
Barwell
Pope   —   dishonest
Thynne U.O. 1 2 3
Williams R.V. 1.2 3   } noisy
Mendel   1. 2. 3

Detail of 'Extra School' book,
19 February 1887

After two years in the house of Dr Haig Brown (the headmaster) Ralph moved to the house of the school organist, Mr G. H. Robinson, and spent his last four terms as Head of the House. He took part in games and other school activities but preferred walks and half-holiday expeditions.

Hervey. 1887

Ralph. 1888

Meggie. 1888

There was a great deal of music making during the holidays. Hervey played the cello, Meggie the piano, and Ralph the violin or viola. When they all stayed with their cousins at Bournemouth or at Gunby Hall in Lincolnshire, or had other friends to stay, Ralph arranged music for whatever instruments were available.

During the summer of 1890, the year Ralph left Charterhouse, he heard Die Walküre *in Munich and became enthralled by Wagner's music.*

Ralph entered the Royal College of Music in September 1890. After two terms he was allowed to study composition with Hubert Parry who was a composer of wide interests, an early champion of Wagner, an admirer of Ibsen, and a scholar as well as a musician. He lent scores to his pupils and showed Ralph the greatness of Bach and Beethoven. 'Parry,' Ralph said, 'was a thinker on music, which he connected not only with life, but with other aspects of art and science.' The influence of such thought, as well as Parry's friendship and kindness, opened new worlds for Ralph. When in 1892 Ralph went to Trinity College, Cambridge, he continued to go to London for weekly lessons with Parry. He studied with Charles Wood at Cambridge, 'the finest technical instructor I have ever known,' and took organ lessons from Alan Gray. He took part in the musical life of the University and continued to compose, though his main study was history in which he took a good degree the year after he had passed his Mus.B. He had friendly Darwin cousins living at Cambridge, and another cousin and contemporary, Ralph Wedgwood, introduced him to a number of fellow undergraduates with lively minds and great talents. Among them were the Llewelyn Davies brothers, the two younger Trevelyans, Maurice Amos, G. E. Moore, and Eddie Marsh. Hugh Allen, a fellow member of the University Musical Club, conducted one of Ralph's songs at a concert, and Ralph himself conducted a small choral society. Besides music there were tennis parties, bicycling expeditions, skating in winter, many dances, and all the other pleasures of being young in congenial society. At Cambridge he met again some of the Fisher family. Florence had married a young and brilliant historian, F. W. Maitland, and her sister Adeline often stayed with them. Florence would invite Ralph, and other young musicians,

Ivor and Nicholas Gatty, to play chamber music with her, Adeline playing piano or cello as required.

Ralph returned to the Royal College of Music in 1895. Here, too, he was fortunate in his contemporaries, among them were Dunhill, Ireland, Howard-Jones, and Fritz Hart, as well as Gustav Holst. It was in those days at the Royal College of Music that Ralph and Gustav formed the habit of showing each other their work, helping and supporting each other through all their musical difficulties and problems. It was a friendship they needed and valued throughout their lives.

The Royal College of Music was founded in 1882 and incorporated in 1883. The building now belongs to The Royal College of Organists.

Above One of the singing classrooms
above right A violin classroom

Ralph. 1890

Sir George Grove (1820-1900), the first Director of the Royal College of Music, was an engineer, traveller, scholar, and writer before he devoted the greater part of his time to music. He edited the Dictionary of Music and Musicians *and he encouraged a wide interest in all the arts and sciences, believing that an educated mind would best serve the art of Music.*

Friends and contemporaries at Cambridge.

Theodore Llewelyn Davies
Crompton Llewelyn Davies

Ralph Wedgwood

Eddie Marsh
Robert Calverley Trevelyan

Trinity College Cambridge

Reading party at Seatoller. 1895
drawn by Maurice Amos for the Log Book

'*G.M.T.* (coupled with) *Posterity.*
To these two names these pages are
dedicated by the writers.
The one, that of him who granted the first
charter of our liberties, and made over the
territory upon whose border.
Reader, you stand.
By Posterity, whom can we mean,
if not our After-Selves?
Can we hope
that they may have a certain charity for the
Authors?'

from the Log Book

below The house at Seatoller. 1968

The Reading Party
Ralph Vaughan Williams and Ralph
Wedgwood

George Macaulay Trevelyan

George E. Moore

Maurice Amos

When Ralph returned to the Royal College of Music in 1895 Sir George Grove had retired and his successor as Director was Hubert Parry. Ralph went to Charles Stanford for composition lessons.

The Library at the Royal College of Music

Sir Hubert Parry

Sir Charles Stanford

While he was at the Royal College of Music Ralph lived in lodgings in London. He had a small job as organist at the church of St Barnabas, South Lambeth. Here he tried to form a choral society and here he learned the deficiencies of the musical life of most small churches. It was a job he did not enjoy, and he was glad to leave the work to a deputy when he married Adeline Fisher in October 1897. They went to Berlin for several months, and there Ralph studied composition with Max Bruch. They spent Christmas at San Remo, a few more weeks in Berlin, and visited Dresden and Prague before returning to London. Once settled they saw much of Ralph's Cambridge and College friends. In 1898 Ralph passed his FRCO examination and a year later that for his Cambridge Mus D. He gave up St Barnabas with great thankfulness—the new vicar did not care to have an agnostic organist—and earned his living by writing, teaching, and giving University Extension Lectures. He was writing music, and during the first years of the century Dan Godfrey with the Bournemouth Symphony Orchestra gave performances of his works.

During these years Adeline was much absorbed by the care of an invalid brother, and by the anguish of her closely knit family circle when another brother returned shell-shocked from the Boer war and, after months of illness, died.

Ralph edited a volume of Purcell's Welcome songs for the Purcell society, undertook the musical editorship of *The English Hymnal*, and started to collect folk-songs, reflecting his delighted discovery of a musical tradition that had as deep an influence on him as the work of the great Tudor composers.

On 9 October 1897 Ralph married Adeline Fisher. The families were old friends: Ralph's father and Adeline's had known each other as undergraduates at Oxford. Ralph and Adeline spent their honeymoon in Berlin, where Ralph studied composition with Max Bruch. They spent a Christmas holiday at San Remo, where Adeline's family were staying.

Ralph and Adeline
Ralph

Ralph with one of his brothers-in-law
Ralph at Bolzano. Photographed by Adeline.

When Ralph and Adeline returned to London they lived in various furnished rooms until 1899 when they moved into 10 Barton Street, Westminster. Ralph gave University Extension lectures and wrote articles for The Vocalist, *but he was able to spend most of his time composing, and the Barton Street address appears on all his manuscripts written during the next six years.*

top The Vicarage,
Hooton Roberts
above Croquet at
Hooton Roberts

Ralph had known Nicholas and Ivor Gatty at
Cambridge. Another brother, René, had been in
Berlin whilst he and Adeline were there and had
become a great friend; their father was the vicar of
Hooton Roberts in Yorkshire where Ralph and
Adeline spent many holidays.

top left Adeline
top right Ralph
above Rough music at
Hooton Roberts

Nicholas Gatty played the violin, Ivor the horn, and Ralph the viola, while the music was arranged by either Ralph or Nicholas for whatever instruments were available. The Gattys' young sister, Margot, was also a violinist, and Adeline played the piano as well as the cello ; so there was plenty of variety.

Adeline 1908

Principal works

1904 *Symphonic Rhapsody* unpublished, destroyed. First performance, Bournemouth, 7 March 1904
The House of Life
Songs of Travel
French folk-song arrangements

1905 Music for the Masque *Pan's Anniversary*
Songs, words by Tennyson and Christina Rossetti
Edited Purcell Society Vol XV

1906 Publication of *The English Hymnal*
Norfolk Rhapsodies Nos. I, II, and III

1907 *Toward the Unknown Region*

1908 Publication of *Folk Songs from the Eastern Counties*
Songs, words by Hardy and Verlaine

1909 *On Wenlock Edge*
Incidental music for *The Wasps*
A Sea Symphony (First performed 1910)

1910 *Fantasia on English Folk Songs*
Edited Purcell Society Vol XVIII
Fantasia on a theme by Thomas Tallis

1911 *Five Mystical Songs*

1912 *Phantasy Quintet*
Fantasia on Christmas Carols
Folk Songs for Schools (arrangements)

1913 *O Praise the Lord of Heaven* Anthem
Five English Folk Songs
A London Symphony (First performed 1914)
Incidental music for plays at Stratford-upon-Avon

13 Cheyne Walk. Ralph and Adeline lived here from 1905 until 1929

SOLOISTS:

MISS B. BOOKER (Soprano).   MR. J. FRANCIS HARFORD (Bass).
MRS. RONALD CARTER (Violin).   MISS MARY CRACROFT (Piano).
ACCOMPANIST—MR. HENRY BIRD.
CONDUCTOR—DR. R. VAUGHAN WILLIAMS.

THE CHORUS is formed by the following CHORAL SOCIETIES—

ABINGER.   CAPEL.   SHALFORD.
ALBURY.   COLDHARBOUR.   SHERE.
WESTCOTT.

✳ ✳ PROGRAMME. ✳ ✳

PART I.

Selection from "Judas Maccabæus," ... ... *Handel.*

OVERTURE.

—o—

CHORUS.

O Father Whose Almighty pow'r
The heav'ns, and earth, and seas adore,
The hearts of Judah, Thy delight,
In one defensive band unite,
And grant a leader bold and brave
If not to conquer, born to save.

RECIT. AND AIR (BASS).

I feel the Deity within,
Who the bright Cherubin between,
His radiant glory, erst display'd,
To Israel's distressful pray'r,
He hath vouchsaf'd a gracious ear,
And points out Maccabæus to their aid.
Judas shall set the captive free,
And lead us on to victory.

Arm, arm, ye brave; a noble cause,
The cause of Heav'n your zeal demands;
In defence of your nation, religion, and laws,
The Almighty Jehovah will strengthen your hands.

CHORUS.

We come, we come, in bright array,
Judah, thy sceptre to obey.

AIR (SOPRANO).

Come ever smiling Liberty,
And with thee bring thy jocund train;
For thee we pant and sigh, for thee
With whom eternal pleasures reign.

CHORUS.

Lead on, lead on, Judah disdains
The galling load of hostile chains.

RECIT. AND AIR (SOPRANO).

O let eternal honours crown his name,
Judas, first Worthy in the rolls of fame;
Say " He put on the breast plates as a giant,
" And girt his warlike harness about him.
" In his acts he was like a lion,
" And like a lion's whelp roaring for his prey."

From mighty Kings he took the spoil,
And with his acts made Judah smile.
Judah rejoiceth in his name,
And triumphs in her hero's fame.

AIR (BASS).

The Lord worketh wonders
His glory to raise,
And still as he thunders,
Is fearful in praise.

MARCH.

SEMI-CHORUS.

See the conquering hero comes,
Sound the trumpets, beat the drums;
Sports prepare, the laurel bring,
Songs of triumph to him sing.
See the godlike youth advance,
Breathe the flutes and lead the dance;
Myrtle wreaths and roses twine,
To deck the hero's brow divine.

CHORUS.

See the conquering hero comes,
Sound the trumpets, beat the drums;
Sports prepare, the laurel bring,
Songs of triumph to him sing.

Lady Farrer, who had been a fellow pupil of Ralph's at the Royal College of Music in 1890, and Meggie Vaughan Williams founded the Leith Hill Musical Festival. Ralph was the Festival conductor until 1953.

left The programme of the first Leith Hill Musical Festival. 1905

below Meggie Vaughan Williams, first Secretary of the Festival.

THE LATE SECRETARY
F. R. SPARK   IN THE AUDIENCE

MR. H. H. PICKARD, CHORUS PIANIST
IN THE AUDIENCE

SIR HUBERT PARRY.

SIR CHARLES STANFORD

'DR. VAUGHAN WILLIAMS
CONDUCTING HIS
"SEA SYMPHONY"

MADAME CLARA BUTT.

M. RACHINAMINOFF.

MR CAMPBELL McINNES.

Toward the Unknown Region, *a setting for chorus and orchestra of a poem by Walt Whitman, had its first performance which Ralph conducted at the Leeds Festival in 1907. In 1910 he conducted the Sea Symphony, a choral symphony with a text chosen from poems by Whitman which had taken him seven years to compose, on his thirty-eighth birthday. The soloists were Cicely Gleeson White and Campbell McInnes and the work is dedicated to Ralph Wedgwood.*

Gustav Holst in his music room. 1910

Ever since their meeting as students at the Royal College of Music in 1895 Ralph and Gustav had been friends. They discussed and criticized each other's compositions, and they gave each other every support in all musical undertakings. Holst devoted much of his time to teaching. In 1905 he became Musical Director of St Paul's Girls' School, an appointment he held until the year of his death, and in 1907 he became Musical Director of Morley College for Working Men and Women.

Ralph about 1910

George Butterworth (1885-1916) was a younger friend whose company Ralph enjoyed, and whose music he admired. They made some arduous and hilarious expeditions collecting folk-songs in the eastern counties of England.

Principal works

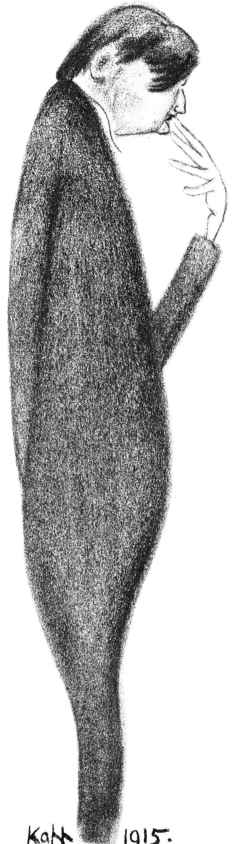

1914 *Four Hymns* for tenor, viola obbligato, and orchestra

1915 No works were published
1916

1917 *Selected Folk Songs* arranged for voice and pianoforte by Cecil Sharp and RVW. (This may have belonged to the pre-war years.)

1919 Arrangements of songs contributed to *The Motherland Song Books*, Nos. I, II, III, and IV
Eight Traditional English Carols arranged for voice and pianoforte

1920 *Three Preludes for Organ* founded on Welsh hymn tunes : Bryn Calfaria, Rhosymedre, Hyfrydol
O Clap Your Hands, motet
Twelve Traditional Carols from Herefordshire, collected and arranged by RVW
The Lark Ascending. Romance for violin and orchestra
Suite of Six short pieces for pianoforte ; also arranged for string orchestra as *The Charterhouse Suite*.

1921 *Lord thou hast been our refuge*, motet
Merciless Beauty. Three rondels for high voice and string trio
A Pastoral Symphony (First performance 1922)

1922 *O vos Omnes*, motet
Mass in G minor
The Shepherds of the Delectable Mountains

Kapp 1915.

Cartoon by Kapp

Working party (Ralph extreme left)

In August 1914 Ralph joined the Special Constabulary ; by the end of the month he was a sergeant. A few weeks later he enlisted in the Royal Army Medical Corps.

As a private in the 2/4th London Field Ambulance he underwent training with his unit in the home counties and on Salisbury Plain. During this time he collected and rehearsed groups of singers for informal concerts, played the organ in local churches, both for Church

top 2/4th Field Ambulance Band. Saffron Walden.

above 'Pancreas Place'. 1916 (Harry Steggles standing next to Ralph on left).

Parades and for his own pleasure, and became accompanist to a fellow private, Harry Steggles. Their performance of 'When Father Papered the Parlour' was a favourite at entertainments in camp.
Ralph and Harry Steggles were together throughout the period of training and on active service in both France and Salonica. Ralph relied on the younger soldier's help in many ways, not least in the matter of kit inspection and equipment.

Route March

Motor ambulance at Ecoivres

Horse-drawn ambulance

right Harry Steggles and Ralph with ambulance

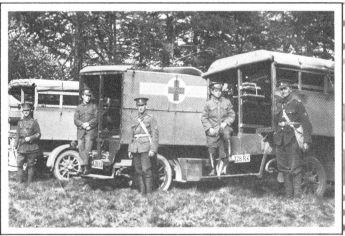

In June 1916 the unit went to France and had its headquarters at Ecoivres, a village below Mont St Eloi, near Arras. The dressing station was in the outbuildings of a large house. Ralph went up to the front lines in an ambulance to collect the wounded, usually in the evening. He said that hearing a bugler practising gave him the first idea for his Pastoral Symphony.

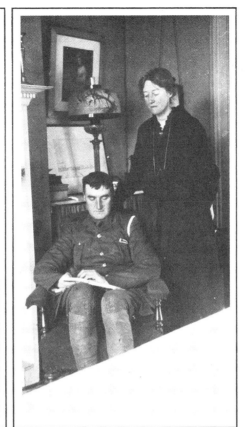

NOTHING is to be written on this side except the date and signature of the sender. Sentences not required may be erased. If anything else is added the post card will be destroyed.

I am quite well.

I have been admitted into hospital
{ sick } and am going on well.
{ wounded } and hope to be discharged soon.

I am being sent down to the base.

I have received your { letter dated
{ telegram „
{ parcel

Letter follows at first opportunity.

I have received no letter from you
{ lately
{ for a long time.

A MERRY X MAS

Signature } R. V. Williams
only

Date Dec 6ᵗʰ 1916

[Postage must be prepaid on any letter or post card addressed to the sender of this card.]

far left Field postcard

Ralph, on leave, with Adeline at Cheyne Walk. 1917

Ralph's mother at Leith Hill Place. 1917

Ralph. 1919

*In 1916 Ralph's unit was sent to Salonica where they spent a cold
winter on the hills below Mount Olympus. There was little to do and
Ralph was restive. He was able to return to England to be trained for a
commission. In 1918 he returned to France as a subaltern in 141 Heavy
Battery, Royal Garrison Artillery, on active service. After the
Armistice he was made Director of Music, First Army, British
Expeditionary Force in France. In February 1919 he was demobilized.*

top left Ralph conducting the Leith Hill Musical Festival

top right Ralph and Adeline

above Fancy Dress Ball at the Slade. (Ralph as a sheik, extreme right, front)

Ralph settled down to revise his pre-war opera Hugh the Drover, *to write his* Pastoral Symphony, *and to take up the threads of his musical life. In June 1919 he received a D Mus.* Honoris causa *at Oxford. In the Autumn term he started teaching composition at the Royal College of Music where his friend Hugh Allen had succeeded Hubert Parry as Director.*

Ralph and Gustav Holst both enjoyed walking tours and they would go off for a few days exploring new places or revisiting country they both knew well.

Old King Cole

Hugh the Drover

Ralph was President of the Cambridge branch of the English Folk Dance and Song Society. He wrote for them a ballet, Old King Cole, *first performed at Trinity as part of the Cambridge Festival of 1923.*

The first performance of Hugh the Drover *was by students at the Royal College of Music in July 1924. The first professional performance was given a few days later by the British National Opera Company conducted by Malcolm Sargent.*

Ralph. 1920

Gustav Holst. 1920

right Ralph. 1921
far right Gustav Holst. 1921

Rehearsing at the Royal Opera House. *(Left to right)* Eugene Goossens, Major Oliver Bernard, Percy Pitt (Director of the British National Opera Company), and Gustav Holst at the piano.

In 1921 Ralph succeeded Sir Hugh Allen as Musical Director of the Bach Choir. He was delighted because it gave him an opportunity of working with an excellent chorus, engaging the best soloists and having a professional orchestra to conduct in performances of music he loved.

By 1923 Gustav Holst's music was being performed in both England and America. The Covent Garden Season opened with his opera, The Perfect Fool, *conducted by Eugene Goossens.*

Principal works

1923 *Old King Cole*, ballet for orchestra and chorus
English Folk Songs, suite for military band
Sea Songs, quick march for military and brass bands
Let us now praise famous men, unison song

1924 *Toccata Marziale* for military band
Hugh the Drover

1925 Songs:
Two poems by Seumas O'Sullivan
Three Songs from Shakespeare
Four poems by Fredegond Shove
Three poems by Walt Whitman
Flos Campi
Sancta Civitas
Concerto in D Minor (*Concerto Accademico*) for violin and orchestra
Magnificat and Nunc Dimittis (The village service)
Hymn tunes in *Songs of Praise*. The music editors were RVW and Martin Shaw

1926 *Six studies in English Folk Song* for violoncello and pianoforte
On Christmas Night

1927 *Along the Field*. Eight Housman songs for voice and violin

1928 Te Deum in G
The Oxford Book of Carols. Edited by Percy Dearmer, RVW, and Martin Shaw
Sir John in Love. (First performance 1929)

1929 *Benedicite* for soprano, chorus, and orchestra
The Hundredth Psalm
Three Choral Hymns
Fantasia on Sussex Folk Tunes for violoncello and orchestra
Hymn Prelude on Song 13 by Orlando Gibbons

1930 *Job*. A Masque for dancing

1931 *Concerto in C major* for pianoforte and orchestra

1932 *Magnificat*

1933 Revised Edition of *The English Hymnal*
The Running Set

1934 *Fantasia on Greensleeves*
Anthem, *O how Amiable*
Suite for Viola and small orchestra
Folk Songs from Newfoundland
Symphony in F Minor (No. 4) (First performance 1935)

1935 Folk-Song arrangements
Five Tudor Portraits

1936 *Nothing is here for tears*, choral song
The Poisoned Kiss
Riders to the Sea
Dona Nobis Pacem

1937 *Flourish for a Coronation*
Festival Te Deum

Ralph as audience

Sir Hugh Allen

48

above Ralph with a Morris dancer
above right Gustav Holst

Dorothy Longman, wife of Ralph's great friend R. G. Longman, was a fine amateur violinist. Vally Lasker and Nora Day were on the music staff of St Paul's Girls' School and both gave the greatest help to Ralph and Gustav in playing through new works.

THE THREE CHOIRS FESTIVAL AT GLOUCESTER

The Triennial Musical Festival at Gloucester has, as usual, been favoured with brilliant weather, and nearly all the prominent stars of the musical world of England have been present.

1.—Sir Edward Elgar well wrapped up on Monday, when he conducted rehearsals of his works.

2.—Mr. Geo. Bernard Shaw, wearing a steward's badge, leaving the Cathedral on Wednesday.

3.—Mr. W. H. Reed (left), leader of orchestra and solo violinist, with Mr. H. W. Sumsion, organist of Cathedral.

4.—Miss Elsie Suddaby (solo soprano) (left) and Miss Muriel Brunskill (solo contralto) (right).

5.—Dr. Percy Hull, organist of Hereford Cathedral.

6.—Mr. Horace Stevens (solo bass) and Mr. Heddle Nash (solo tenor) at the "Elijah" performance.

7.—Dr. Vaughan Williams, the composer.

8.—Sir Ivor Atkins and Sir Walford Davies in front. Col. Frank Isaac, of Worcester, behind.

9.—Mr. A. F. Watts and Dr. Lee Williams.

10.—Mr. S. A. Pitcher and Professor Herbert Howells.

11.—Mrs. Croft and Miss Doris Leach.

("Cheltenham Chronicle" Photos. Copies 1s. and 1s. 9d. each.

50

top right The White
Gates
top left The Gate
above Haymaking in
the field behind the
house

*Adeline had become increasingly troubled by arthritis
and found the many stairs at 13 Cheyne Walk
increasingly difficult to manage. So in 1929 she and
Ralph moved to the White Gates, Dorking. Ralph
resigned as Musical Director of the Bach Choir but
continued to teach at the Royal College of Music.*

top left Ralph and Adeline

above Ralph

top right Haymaking. 1934
Robert de Ropp, Elizabeth Darbishire,
Ralph, Naomi Lawrence, Molly Darbishire
Ruth Dyson

above Ralph and Elizabeth Darbishire

Riding

left Outside the study window at the White
Gates
right At the opening of Cecil Sharp House

*Cecil Sharp died in 1924. In 1930 the building that
was to commemorate his great work of collecting the
songs and dances of the English people was completed
and was opened by Adeline's brother, the historian
H. A. L. Fisher. He, as Minister of Education, was
largely responsible for the introduction of this music
to schools.*

53

Ralph had received the gold medal of the Royal Philharmonic Society at a concert in March 1930, when it was presented to him by Arthur Bliss. In April it was his turn to make the presentation to Gustav Holst on behalf of the Society.

Gustav Holst with the Royal Philharmonic Society gold medal

GH

G H singing in the garden of the Bishop's Palace at Chichester

RVW

In 1931 Holst's Whitsuntide Singers, a group made up from his students at Morley College and pupils from St Paul's Girls' School, met in Chichester Cathedral to sing the Mass *Ralph had dedicated to them. There was some less formal music-making out of doors as well.*

left Three Choirs Festival, Hereford. 1933 *(Back)* Alexander Brent Smith, George Dyson, Ralph. *(Front)* Dr Herbert Sumsion of Gloucester, Sir Percy Hull of Hereford, Sir Ivor Atkins of Worcester
below With Ernest Willoughby at Bryn Mawr

With W. H. Reed (leader of the London Symphony Orchestra, 1912-35) at a Three Choirs Festival

Ralph at Bryn Mawr

Ralph and Adeline had visited America in 1922. In 1932 Ralph went to Bryn Mawr College where he gave a series of lectures, later published as National Music.

Three Choirs Festival, Gloucester. 1937

(*left to right*) Lady Rothenstein,
Herbert Howells, Ralph, Rutland
Boughton, Mrs Winterbotham, Sir
William Rothenstein, Mrs Rutland
Boughton, John Sumsion.

centre Ralph and Hervey
left With Adrian Boult
right With Judge Gordon Clark

*In 1935 King George V conferred the Order of Merit on Ralph. To
celebrate this, Lady Farrer gave a party at Abinger Hall.*

Principal works

1938 *England's Pleasant Land*, Pageant
Serenade to Music
Double Trio for string sextet. This was
withdrawn and rewritten as *Partita for
double string orchestra*. 1948
The Bridal Day, masque

1939 Services in D minor
Five Variants of Dives and Lazarus
Suite for pipes

1940 *Six Choral Songs* to be sung in time of war
Motet, *Valiant for Truth*
Music for the film *Forty-Ninth Parallel*
Household Music

1941 *England my England*, choral song

1942 Music for the film *Coastal Command*
Nine Carols for male voices
Incidental Music for *Pilgrim's Progress*,
broadcast version

1943 *Symphony in D Major* (No. 5)
Music for the film *The People's Land*
Music for the film *Flemish Farm*

1944 *Concerto in A minor* for oboe and strings
String quartet in A minor. for Jean on her
birthday
Thanksgiving for Victory (Broadcast
13 May 1945)
Music for the film *The Stricken Peninsula*

1945 Chant for Psalm 67 *Deus Miseratur*

1946 *Introduction and Fugue* for two pianofortes
Music for the film *The Loves of Joanna
Godden*

Ralph, *c.* 1930

Hervey, *c.* 1930

right Tennis at Quaker's Orchard
far right Piper's Guild Summer School at
Bishop Otter College, Chichester. 1939

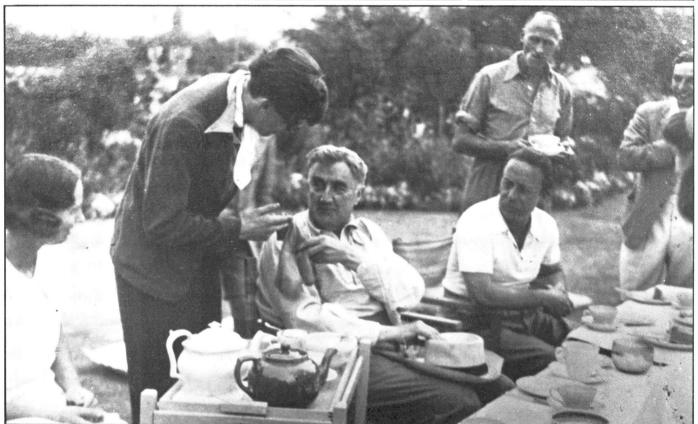

Conductors' Conference at Quaker's
Orchard (Sir Adrian and Lady Boult's
house), Peaslake. 1938

(Left to right) Lady Boult, Bernard Rose,
Ralph, Clarence Raybould, Saunders Jacks,
Michael Porter

Conducting the band of the 2nd Battalion of the Duke of Cornwall's Light Infantry at Milton Court, Dorking, for the performance of a pageant-play, *England's Pleasant Land,* written by E. M. Forster in aid of the Dorking Preservation Society. The incidental music was written by several composers. In the music which Ralph had written for two of the episodes, he used material which was later to become part of his Fifth Symphony.

top left Ralph wrote a *Te Deum* for the Coronation of King George VI. He attended the ceremony wearing the robes of a Doctor of Music of the University of Cambridge; these had been left to him by his old friend and teacher, Alan Gray, who had inherited them from the great organist Thomas Walmisley (1814-56). These robes are now in the possession of Trinity College, Cambridge.

top right Ralph received an Honorary Doctorate of Music at Trinity College, Dublin, in June 1939.
(Left to right) James Sullivan Starkie (Seamus O'Sullivan), Ralph, and George H. P. Hewson, Professor of Music at Trinity College, Dublin.

Ursula Wood 1935. She and Ralph met in March 1938 to discuss a libretto she had written. This eventually became the masque Epithalamion, *based on Spenser's poem, for which Ralph wrote the music the following winter.*

R.V.W. *1938*

right Ralph wrote his *Serenade to Music* as a tribute to Sir Henry Wood for a concert to celebrate his Jubilee as a conductor, 5 October 1938. On 3 March 1944, Sir Henry's 75th birthday, Ralph made a presentation to him on behalf of the Performing Right Society.

far right R. O. Morris (1886-1948), musical scholar, teacher, and composer, also author of many of the crossword puzzles published by *The Times*. He married Adeline's elder sister, Emmeline Fisher, in 1915. After her death in 1941 he remained at the White Gates until the end of the war.

Sir Stanley Marchant (1883-1949), Principal of the Royal Academy of Music, seen with Ralph at a meeting of the Council for the Encouragement of Music and the Arts Music Panel, of which Sir Stanley was the Chairman.

top left With Harry Steggles at the White Gates.

top right The spire of St Martin's Church, Dorking, seen from the orchard at the White Gates.

above left Ralph with Jean Stewart, the viola player (for whom he wrote his Quartet in A minor), outside St Martin's Church.

above right With the composer Gerald Finzi and Isidore Schwiller, who led the orchestra for the Leith Hill Musical Festivals from 1908 to 1954

During the war the Dorking Halls, built for the Leith Hill Musical Festival, was used as a government store. So Ralph conducted many concerts in St Martin's church.

Leith Hill Place,
the north front

Hervey Vaughan Williams died in 1944, leaving Leith Hill Place to Ralph, who gave it to the National Trust. The Trust's first tenants, to Ralph's great pleasure, were his cousin Ralph Wedgwood with his wife Iris.

Principal works

1947   *The souls of the righteous*, motet
Symphony in E Minor (No. 6) (First
performance 1948)

1948   *Prayer to the Father of Heaven*, motet
Music for the film *Scott of the Antarctic*

1949   *Folk Songs of the Four Seasons*
An Oxford Elegy
Fantasia quasi variazione *on the Old 104th
Psalm tune*
Music for the film *Dim Little Island*

1950   *Concerto Grosso*
Music for the film *Bitter Springs*
Sons of Light
Incidental music for radio serial *The Mayor
of Casterbridge*

Painting by William Narraway

Opposite page
top left The Leith Hill Musical Festival, 1947,
in the re-opened Dorking Halls.
left Ralph at the Royal Albert Hall, where he
conducted many of his own works.

With Foxy, one of the longest-lived, most intelligent and favourite of Ralph's succession of cats.

(Left to right, back row) Mrs Archer, Sir F Ogilvie, Edmund Rubbra, Sir J. Westrup, Gerald Finzi, Dr H. K. Andrews

(Front row) Joseph Colegrove,
Dr S. Watson,
Dr P. Peacock,
Ralph,
Dr Emily Daymond,
Lady Ponsonby,
Sir William Harris,
Dr Thomas Armstrong.

Sir Hubert Parry's centenary, 12 May 1948, was celebrated during the Oxford Festival of Music by a concert in the Sheldonian. Ralph's Prayer to the Father of Heaven *(Skelton) was a tribute written for the occasion and sung by the Oxford Bach Choir conducted by Thomas Armstrong.*

Three Choirs Festival, Gloucester, 1950
top With *(left to right)* Frederick Thurston
(who gave the first performance of Gerald
Finzi's Clarinet Concerto), Nigel Finzi,
Gerald Finzi, and Christopher Finzi
above, with Richard Latham, Jean Stewart,
and Ursula Wood.

top Three Choirs Festival, Hereford, 1949.

above At the White Gates with Myles and
Cedric Glover and Dr Douglas Fox

At the wedding of Sir Adrian Boult's step-daughter, Margaret Wilson. 1949

below Presenting the Royal Philharmonic Society's gold medal to Sir John Barbirolli. 14 December 1950

Principal works

1951   *The Pilgrim's Progress.* A Morality
Three Shakespeare songs
Romance for harmonica and orchestra

1952   *Sinfonia Antartica* (No. 7) (First performance 1953)
O taste and see, motet written for the coronation of Queen Elizabeth II

1953   *Silence and Music*, partsong

Opposite page
Ralph in the big room at the White Gates.
1951. Adeline, seen on the right, wearing
an eyeshade, died on 10 May 1951

The study, the White Gates. Summer 1951

The Pilgrim's Progress, a Morality, was staged at the Royal Opera House, Covent Garden. 26 April 1951

Rehearsal with the conductor, Leonard Hancock

During rehearsals

With Leonard Hancock at the first performance

top Conducting the Ministry of Education's
teachers' course at Lodge Hill, Pulborough,
Sussex. 1952

left With H.M. Inspectors of Schools, *(left
to right)* Raymond Roberts, M. Crozier,
Gerald Trodd, Elsie Smith, Ralph, Bernard
Shore.

below Bernard Shore, Ivor James (cellist),
Ralph, Ursula Wood

At the White Gates. Summer 1952

right In Leith Hill Woods

top Dr Walter Stanton presenting Ralph to
the Chancellor
After the ceremony: Mr A. E. Russell, Ralph,
Lord Camrose, the Rt. Hon. James Chuter
Ede, Admiral Sir Philip Vian, the Chancellor,
Gen. Lord Ismay, Sir Charles Lillicrap,
Sir Philip Morris

*On 14 December 1951 Ralph received, from the
hands of the Chancellor, Mr Winston Churchill, the
first Honorary Doctorate of Music given by the
University of Bristol.*

The Oxford Orchestral Society's Jubilee Concert. 14 June 1952
After a performance of *The Serenade to Music* in the Sheldonian

below With the conductors: Reginald Jacques, Sidney Watson, Thomas Armstrong, Guy Warrack

right At Chartres.
far right At Mont St Michel.

In May 1952, though the travel allowance was only £25, Ralph took his first holiday abroad since the war.

right At Llanthony Abbey near Hereford, during the Three Choirs Festival. September

far right Leaving Westminster Abbey after the Stanford Centenary Service. 30 September 1952

Ralph wrote a Romance for Harmonica and Orchestra *for Larry Adler which had its first performance at a Promenade Concert on 6 September 1952.*

Replying to the speech made in his honour by Dr Herbert Howells
left to right Lady Ravensdale, Sir John Barbirolli, Ralph, Evelyn Rothwell (Lady Barbirolli)

With C. Day Lewis

The Incorporated Society of Musicians gave a dinner at the Trocadero Restaurant on 7 October 1952 to celebrate Ralph's eightieth birthday.

With Agnes Nicholls (Lady Harty). Ralph
had been a member of the chorus in a
performance of *Dido and Aeneas* in 1895 at
the Royal College of Music when she sang
Dido

With Sir Arthur Bliss

*On Ralph's birthday, 12 October 1952, Sir Adrian
Boult conducted at the Royal Festival Hall a
programme of Ralph's works,* A Song of Thanksgiving, 5th Symphony, Flos Campi, *and* The Sons
of Light. *It was followed by a party given by the
London County Council.*

Sinfonia Antartica. First performance, Manchester. 14 January 1953

above With Peter Scott (son of Captain Scott of the Antarctic) and Ursula Wood

right On the platform of the Free Trade Hall after the performance

Opposite page
top Ralph with the Hallé Orchestra in the rehearsal room at Manchester

foot Sinfonia Antartica. A rehearsal at the Free Trade Hall for the first performance conducted by Sir John Barbirolli.

With Roy Douglas at a rehearsal

After the performance, with Ernest Irving to whom the work is dedicated

The first London performance of the Sinfonia Antartica, *Royal Festival Hall, 21 January 1953 by the Hallé Orchestra was conducted by Sir John Barbirolli.*

Principal works

1954 *Concerto in F minor* for bass tuba and
orchestra
This Day (Hodie)
Sonata in A minor for violin and pianoforte
Songs:
Heart's Music
Menelaus on the Beach at Pharos

1955 *Prelude on Three Welsh Hymn Tunes*, for
brass band
Symphony (No. 8) *in D minor* (First
performance 1956)
Music for the film *The England of Elizabeth*

Crispin and Friskin, kittens given as a
moving-in present by Gerald and Joyce
Finzi

The party at Nottingham. At the table
Ursula Vaughan Williams, Ralph, and Mary
Bourne; behind, Benjamin Britten, Peter
Pears, and John Kentish

Ralph conducted the first public performance of his *Prelude on an old Carol Tune*
(founded on incidental music written for
the broadcast serialization of *The Return of
the Native* by Thomas Hardy) at King's
Lynn Festival on 31 July 1953
London rehearsal, with the Boyd Neel
Orchestra, for King's Lynn

In October there was an amateur performance of
Hugh the Drover *at Nottingham. At the party
afterwards Benjamin Britten and Peter Pears, who
had been giving a recital that evening, were fellow
guests, as were the professional singers, Mary Bourne
and John Kentish, who took the principal parts in the
opera.*

Sir Gilmour Jenkins

Hanover Terrace 1953 (Nos. 10 and 11 are
under the pediment)

*Ralph Vaughan Williams and Ursula Wood were
married in February 1953. They moved to
10 Hanover Terrace, Regent's Park. Ralph's best
man at the wedding, who sang Pilate in the Dorking
Bach Choir's performances of Bach's St John Passion,
was Sir Gilmour Jenkins, Permanent Secretary of
the Ministry of Transport.*

Holiday in Italy.
May 1953

With Gerald Finzi
at the Three Choirs
Festival, Gloucester.
1953

far left Gypsy Hill Training College, Summer School of Music. 1953. Norman and Violet Askew, Ralph, Anne MacNaghton, Margaret Major, Elizabeth Rajna, and David Stone

Three Choirs Festival, Worcester. 1954
left With Herbert Howells and Leslie Woodgate
below With Herbert Howells and David Willcocks (then Organist of Worcester Cathedral)

Three Choirs Festival, Worcester. 1954
top Rehearsing in the Cathedral
above The choristers who sang the narration in the first performance of Ralph's new work, *Hodie*

top Rehearsing in the Cathedral, with David Willocks
above With Canon and Mrs Briggs, with whom Ralph was staying as he had done for many years when the Festival was at Worcester

right Conducting the Cornell Symphony
Orchestra at a rehearsal

below By the swimming pool at the
Biltmore Hotel, Santa Barbara, California

right With the cast of *Riders to the Sea* in
the Biltmore Hotel garden. Carl Zytowski
(Director of the Opera Theater, University
of California), Warren Sherlock, Charles
Farlee, Betty-Carol Gilbert, Ralph,
Jean Cook, and Shirely Sproule

*Directly after the Three Choirs Festival, 1954, Ralph took up a
visiting professorship at Cornell University for the Autumn term.
Keith Falkner, at that time on the University's music staff, arranged
a lecture tour that took Ralph right across the continent. He also
conducted, while at Cornell, both the University Orchestra and the
Buffalo Symphony Orchestra.*

right Rehearsal at Buffalo. With the
conductor Josef Krips

below After the concert at Buffalo:
Mrs Charles E. Mott, Ursula, Ralph, and
Hans Vigeland, Organist and Choirmaster

Luther Noss, Dean of the Yale School of
Music, with A. Whitney Griswold, President
of Yale University, presenting the prize

*Before leaving America in December 1954, Ralph
received the Howland Memorial prize and Medal at
New Haven University. He was the third composer
to receive the award, the others being Gustav Holst
(1925) and Paul Hindemith (1940).*

above In London with General Wilfrid
Kitching, Lieut. Col. Bernard-Andrews, and
Colonel Albert Jakeway of the Salvation
Army at the Army's headquarters in Judd
Street, after a rehearsal with the Staff Band
of the *Prelude on three Welsh Hymn Tunes*
written for them. February 1955

top Addressing the Annual General
Meeting of the E.F.D.S.S. 1955
above With Douglas Kennedy, Director of
the English Folk Dance and Song Society,
of which Ralph was President

At a party in the Pittville Gardens,
Cheltenham, during the Festival. 1955
(left to right) Michael Kennedy, Eslyn
Kennedy, Stanley Bate (an ex-pupil of
Ralph's whose 3rd Symphony had its first
performance during the Festival), Ralph,
Ursula, and Frank Howes (then Music
Critic of *The Times*)

Holiday in Greece. September 1955
above Pony ride up the hill, Delphi
top right At the temple, Sunion
right Athens: the Acropolis

Returning from Greece, Ralph and Ursula were met by Frank Hollins at Venice. He drove them back across Italy and over the Alps. They spent some days in France, mostly in the valley of the Loire.

right Picnic at the top of the Lauteret pass
far right Picnic in woods in France. Ralph and Frank Hollins

In October Ralph gave the first of the Arnold Bax memorial lectures at the University of Cork

(front row) Professor Aloys Fleishman, Ralph, and Professor John P. Teegan
(back row) Ursula, Mrs Fleishman, and Harriet Cohen

Principal works

1956 *A Vision of Aeroplanes*, motet
Two Organ Preludes

1957 *Epithalamion*
Variations for Brass Band
Flourish for Glorious John
Symphony (No. 9) *in E minor*. (First
performance 1958)
Ten Blake Songs

1958 *Three vocalises*
The First Nowell. A nativity play, with
music composed and arranged by RVW
was left unfinished at his death and
completed by Roy Douglas.

Ralph dedicated his Eighth Symphony to Sir John Barbirolli. The first performance was on 2 May 1956 at the Free Trade Hall, Manchester

At a rehearsal

At a party after the first performance *(left to right)* Sir John, Lady Barbirolli, Ralph, Ursula, and the leader of the Hallé, Laurence Turner

Opposite page
With Sir John Barbirolli at rehearsals

At Hanover Terrace with the South African
composer Arnold Van Wyk

With Professor Wallace Woodworth and Sir
Adrian Boult at a party after the presentation
of medals by the Harvard Glee Club in
London, July 1956

Garden Party at Gloucester during the Festival, with George Hannam Clark (the actor, whom Ralph had known as a member of Benson's company when he had been musical adviser at Stratford in 1912), David Willcocks and Ursula

The house party at Gloucester for the Festival. (left to right) Joy Finzi, Gerald Finzi (who died a few weeks later), Harold Browne, Mrs Cunningham, David Willcocks, Christopher Finzi, Howard Ferguson, and Ursula. (back) Nigel Finzi, Meredith Davies, and Richard Shirley-Smith. (front) Ralph

Croquet at the Finzis' house, Ashmansworth

Bust by David McFall. 1956

At the Three Choirs Festival, Gloucester. 1956.

above Conducting at a rehearsal
above centre and right Excursions near
Haddo (Aberdeenshire)
right With some of the choir

Ralph was invited to conduct Parry's Blest Pair of Sirens *at Haddo House before a performance by the Haddo Choral Society of the* Sea Symphony, *conducted by June Gordon (Countess of Haddo). May 1957.*

above left With Leopold Stokowski at
10 Hanover Terrace
above With Alan Frank and Grigor
Piatigorski at the Royal Festival Hall, after
a rehearsal of Sir William Walton's Cello
Concerto. 1957

left With Arthur Benjamin at a meeting of
the directors of the New Opera Company of
which Ralph was President

right Ralph's 85th
birthday concert at the
Royal Festival Hall.
When he came into the
Ceremonial Box the
whole audience rose to
greet him

Opposite page
top left Starting for a
holiday in Austria. 1957
top right After a
rehearsal, with Phyllis
Sellick and Cyril Smith.
September 1957
left At the party following the concert.
12 October 1957

113

right Ralph and Michael Tippett

below Rehearsal of Michael Tippett's 2nd
Symphony, B.B.C. Studio, Maida Vale.
1958. Sir Adrian Boult, Michael Tippett,
Ralph, Ursula, and John Minchinton

With Lionel Tertis
and the 'Tertis Viola'

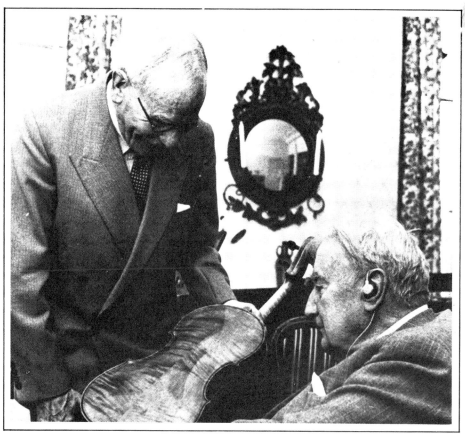

With Herbert Menges
and Lionel Tertis

Following the score

Flos Campi *was played at the 1958 Festival at King's Lynn by Lionel Tertis, for whom Ralph had written it in 1925. He and Herbert Menges came to 10 Hanover Terrace to rehearse with Ralph.*

Rehearsal for the Ninth Symphony at
St Pancras Town Hall, with
Sir Malcolm Sargent and the player of
the flugelhorn, David Mason

In the Ceremonial Box after the first
performance of the Symphony, which is
dedicated to the Royal Philharmonic
Society. Mrs Foggin (wife of Myers Foggin,
Chairman of the Royal Philharmonic
Society), Ursula, Sir Malcolm Sargent and
Mr Ernest Bean, Manager of the Royal
Festival Hall. 2 April 1958

Ursula, Ralph, and Michael Kennedy.
Cheltenham. 17 July 1958.

Ralph died on 26 August 1958. His ashes were buried in Westminster Abbey on 17 September 1958.

Eheu Fugaces
Horace, Odes II. xiv. 1

Swiftly they pass, the flying years,
no prayer can stay their course,
here is the road each man must tread
be he of royal blood or lowly birth.
Vainly we shun the battle's roar
the perilous sea, the fever-laden breezes,
soon shall we reach our journey's end
and trembling cross the narrow stream of death.
Land, house, and wife must all be left,
the cherished trees be all cut down,
strangers shall lord it in our home
and squander all our store.

Translated by Ralph for the Abinger Pageant 1938